# Social Media Marketing

A Beginner's Guide to Dominating the Market with Social Media Marketing

# TABLE OF CONTENTS

Free Marketing Blueprint ........................ v
Chapter 1: Introduction to Social Media Marketing .............................................. 1
Chapter 2: Facebook Marketing for Newbies .................................................... 15
Chapter 3: The Beginner's Guide to Pinterest ..................................................... 31
Chapter 4: Twitter Marketing for Beginners ..................................................... 43
Chapter 5: Instagramming for Social Media Success .................................................. 57
Chapter 6: The Top 14 Instagram Marketing Secrets ................................................. 61
Chapter 7: Cracking the LinkedIn Code ..... 69
Conclusion ........................................... 79
Free Marketing Blueprint ..................... 81
Other Books by Eric J Scott ................... 82

# Free Marketing Blueprint

Marketing can be a complex subject and even after years of experience the same principles still apply.

Give yourself a head start! Grab your free copy of The Marketing Blueprint to help you understand what you need to succeed

To grab your copy of The Marketing Blue Print visit
http://www.mrmarketinghero.com/freebook

# Copyright 2016 by Eric J Scott - All rights reserved.

This document is geared toward providing exact and reliable information in regard to the topic and issue covered. The publication is sold with the idea that the publisher is not required to render accounting, officially permitted, or otherwise, qualified services. If advice is necessary, legal or professional, a practiced individual in the profession should be ordered.

- From a Declaration of Principles which was accepted and approved equally by a Committee of the American Bar Association and a Committee of Publishers and Associations.

In no way is it legal to reproduce, duplicate, or transmit any part of this document in either electronic means or in printed format. Recording of this publication is strictly prohibited and any storage of this document is not allowed unless with written permission from the publisher. All rights reserved.

The information provided herein is stated to be truthful and consistent, in that any liability, in terms of inattention or otherwise, by any usage or abuse of any policies, processes, or directions contained within is the solitary and utter responsibility of the recipient reader. Under no circumstances will any legal responsibility or blame be held against the publisher for any reparation, damages, or monetary loss due to the information herein, either directly or indirectly.

Respective authors own all copyrights not held by the publisher.

The information herein is offered for informational purposes solely, and is universal as so. The presentation of the information is without contract or any type of guarantee assurance.

The trademarks that are used are without any consent, and the publication of the trademark is without permission or backing by the trademark owner. All trademarks and brands within this book are for clarifying purposes only and are owned by the owners themselves, not affiliated with this document.

# Chapter 1

# Introduction to Social Media Marketing

The whole world seems to be caught in a compulsive social media frenzy. Everyone is talking about using social media platforms for engaging their audience, increasing credibility, and building solid brands. There's a marked shift from selling to building relationships, which the social media sites do remarkably well. By definition, social media marketing is nothing but a method of gaining traffic or audience attention for your business through the use of social media. The strategy usually involves concentrating marketing efforts on creating highly engaging content that attracts the attention of your target audience, and encourages them to share it throughout their virtual networks.

Unlike traditional marketing channels, social media marketing doesn't focus on hard selling (though there can be exceptions based on the nature of your business). It is about leveraging the power of audience relationships and forging strong connections through engagement. Social media marketing is about constantly growing your audience base by creating insightful and compelling content. It helps marketers build dramatic brands, fosters customer loyalty, and lays the foundation for selling.

Think of your social media marketing as glamorous toppings on the pizza of your marketing mix. They add more punch and panache to your marketing efforts. Social media marketing makes your marketing techniques more interesting, creative, and appealing to your target audience. It adds a more personal character to your robotic marketing efforts.

Let's take a real life example to establish how social media marketing works. You walk into a department store to buy lipstick or perfume. The salesperson at the counter quickly tries to understand what you want and launches into a tiresome and monotonous script about how XYZ is the bestselling fragrance or lipstick currently. You get frustrated with the whole thing because they are showing you everything that you don't want. The salesperson is not actually helping you buy, but rather trying to sell what they think you should buy. They haven't listened to you or tried to tune in to your requirements. Finally, you move to another store.

At the next store, the salesperson sees you and gives you a warm smile. They chat with you cheerily about your day and the weather. You feel the warmth and friendliness of a real person after talking to them. They take sufficient time to understand exactly what you want by asking you questions related to your lifestyle, preferences and habits. So, do you work very long hours and want a lip color or fragrance that lasts long? Is your style bold, or subtle? Do you enjoy attention, or are you content with toiling diligently in the background?

They talk to you, size you up to understand your needs, and make you feel comfortable. They also offer brilliant tips about how you can make your lipstick last even longer or how certain fragrances can enhance memory and brain functions by stimulating the olfactory glands. In the end, you've had such an enriching experience that you end up buying everything they recommend.

Why? What did the salesperson in the second store do that the one in the first store didn't? They simply connected with you, engaged you in a meaningful conversation, and shared valuable information. Rather than selling you something, they helped you.

Social media marketing is just the same. It is about striking meaningful connections with potential and existing customers to help them buy products and services. Social media marketing is about creating things that excite your customer and makes him think, "Wow, I really want to buy from them." It is about clearing assembly line styles of marketing clutter and replacing it with more personal and relevant messages.

When people like you, they invariably buy from you. Surveys have consistently proved that people buy from brands which they like and can relate to. Before potential customers can turn into loyalists, they need to feel a sense of affinity with your brand. They need to believe your brand values are synonymous with their own. When customers experience a sense of shared belonging with your brand, it won't take much time for them to turn into brand evangelists.

Social media marketing is also significant from the perspective of establishing your authority. It helps you place yourself as an expert in a domain. It reinforces your knowledge and expertise in a specialized niche. Social media marketing lets you position yourself as an influential authority who knows a lot about what you are selling. This automatically increases the credibility and trustworthiness of your brand. People flock to anyone who does justice to the expert tag consistently.

Sharing insightful, thought-provoking, and well-researched matter in your business field makes you come across as someone who is up-to-date with trends within the industry.

Sharp, analytical, and detailed posts present you in a rather flattering light to your target audience. After a while, they start looking forward to your posts on current trends, and they'll engage with you by posing queries and actively soliciting your opinion. All this leads to the creation of an exceptionally credible brand.

Everything else being same (quality and features of product/services etc.), the single most important factor today while making purchasing decisions is customer experience. Customer experience supersedes most other considerations when it comes to buying.

People may compromise on the quality of the product, but they are highly unlikely to overlook an unfavorable customer experience.

Customers like to buy from people who know their material. They prefer buying from sellers who go beyond offering standard products and services and additionally provide slick, new-age value in terms of attractively packaged information and useful tips that make life easier.

Consumers buy from brands they can trust and relate to. Among the hordes of businesses that are trying to garner their attention, customers are most likely to give their money to brands that radiate higher trustworthiness and a personal touch.

Selling is as much about inspiring your buyer's confidence in your brand as it is about extolling the virtues of your products/services. Social media offers you multiple tools, features, and opportunities to do just that – inspire faith in your buyers by building connections through engagement. Let them know you want to help them buy; don't just sell to them.

Social media has traversed far greater heights than simply being a medium for user-generated content. Today, it's a tool for consumer empowerment (we all witness big conglomerates being brought to their knees by that one dissatisfied tweet or widely shared post) and a gratifying brand-consumer partnership.

Even companies that have long been dismissing social media as frivolous and flippant have started taking note of its benefits. They've realized that social media is not limited to games and light-hearted opinion polls (which are also hugely successful in creating affable brands), but can involve more serious discussions and insights that are invaluable when it comes to building strong brands.

One of the best things about social media is that it is amazingly varied and versatile. Some platforms like Pinterest and Instagram are invaluable tools for visually inclined businesses like home décor, cooking, and graphic artists. Meanwhile, channels like LinkedIn and Google+ are ideal for corporate buzz sharing. Twitter and Facebook are flexible enough to be used by businesses of almost all types. With some ingenuity and resourcefulness, even small businesses can create a storm over social media.

Unlike traditional marketing mediums, social media doesn't swallow a huge chunk of your advertising and promotion budget. You don't need to create cost-intensive and ineffectual marketing plans that leave you broke.

All you need is some creativity, perceptiveness, and an intuitive understanding about your audience's needs. More than sharp business acumen, you need a human touch. Social media gives your brand a human angle without breaking the bank.

Have you seen any of the Whole Foods videos posted on their corporate Facebook page? They frequently post how-to videos in a subject that their customers are primarily interested in – cooking. The short videos, running for about 40-60 seconds, cover multiple elements such as animation, images, and text. At the end of the video, there is an item for sale that customers can buy to prepare the recipe mentioned in the video.

One such inventive video demonstrated how customers could transform leftover Thanksgiving turkey into—hold your breath—nachos. What a refreshing change from the same old boring sandwiches! It isn't surprising that these videos are hugely popular and the products mentioned at the end are quickly grabbed up by eager viewers. They must be doing something right!

Rather than using long-winded sales pitches to glorify their products, Whole Foods is adding value to their followers' lives by sharing insanely creative ideas and making life more convenient for them. The company is showing customers ways through which their products can actually benefit them. Ingenious? Yes. Simple? Doubly yes.

Though it seems overwhelmingly complex for a beginner, especially given all the information available over the Internet, social media marketing can be relatively simple and effective.

You really do not have to be a marketing expert to master social media. All you need is some inventiveness, unwavering enthusiasm to keep learning new trends, and an empathetic touch to understand your audience.

Let's do a quick round-up of the benefits of social media marketing.

1. *Enhances Brand Recognition* – Social media gives you endless opportunities to build your brand by increasing visibility. These platforms act as the "voice" of your brand to forge meaningful communication with customers. It serves a two-fold purpose of making your brand look more accessible to prospective customers and making it more familiar for existing customers.

For instance, a regular Facebook user could know about your company by coming across a post in their newsfeed. Similarly, a more non-involved existing customer may turn into a loyal customer after witnessing your powerful presence on several networks.

Put yourself in your customer's shoes. Imagine picking between two similar brands that offer almost the same quality and features. Which one will you pick? The one that has a powerful social presence across platforms or one who hardly engages with customers on social channels?

2. *Increases Brand Loyalty* – A recent report published by Texas Tech University confirms what we all probably know too well by now—brands that engage with customers on social media enjoy greater loyalty. Companies that take advantage of social media tools to connect with their audience are more likely to inspire loyalty and positive buyer connections.

A strategic and flexible social media plan can easily convert new customers into loyal evangelists. A Convince & Convert study recently concluded that 53% of Americans who follow various brands on social media tend to buy from those brands. Obviously, there is direct correlation between social media engagement (yes, even the seemingly frivolous polls, games, and contests) and customer loyalty.

3. *Provides Greater Brand Authority* – Regular engagement with existing customers is a great way to inspire the faith of new customers. When people want to boast about your products and services or applaud you for it, they take to social media.

New members within their circle are attracted enough to follow you. The higher the buzz about your products and services on social media, the more authoritative and credible your brand comes across. If you can engage with other high-ranking brands in the field, your visibility and authority can quickly skyrocket.

4. *Reduces Marketing Costs* – Imagine paying for a thirty-second television advertisement prime time slot (nope, your target audience members are not late television watchers) or hiring outdoor advertising space on a prominent city billboard? How much would that set you back? Probably thousands of dollars, with mostly unimpressive results.

Enter social media marketing. For virtually nothing, you can target customers anywhere on the planet. Creating great content, engaging your audience, driving traffic to your website, and boosting sales conversions isn't cost-heavy on social media platforms. You simply need to be people-savvy, create interesting interactions, and understand how to utilize various tools for optimum benefit.

5. *Raises Search Engine Rankings* – Among other complicated factors search engines use to determine the rank or placement of a web page on their search results, social signals can be one of the most important. When you optimize your posts (with the right keywords, title tags, and meta description) and distribute links pointing to your site throughout social media, you increase your brand signal.

Increased social media activity boosts your authority signal in the eyes of search engines, thus giving you higher rankings on searches when people are actively soliciting products and services related to your niche.

6. *Provides Better Audience Insights* – Few other marketing channels give you the power to target your audience like social media. Businesses can easily target people based on what they follow, their demographics, preferences, and hobbies and interests.

Social media is a great platform from which to gather deeper insights into your customer behavior. Using these insights, you could create products that better suit their compelling needs. Rather than spending astronomical sums targeting all and sundry, hoping and praying that at least some of it yields results, social media allows you to hit the bull's eye.

7. *Improves Customer Service* – Unsurprisingly, a Forbes study revealed that 71% of customers who received a prompt response on social media are more likely to endorse the company's products and services to others.

Social media offer speedy, personal, and direct communication channels for businesses to interact with consumers for problem resolution and other queries.

Unlike other forms of customer service, social media allows other people to view your response in a more open format, thus increasing a brand's transparency and credibility. If you handle an issue faced by a customer remarkably well, you are on your way to earning new customers.

8. *Eases Content Distribution* – Social media dramatically eases the process of content distribution. It can allow you to disseminate your content across a range of platforms to reach a large number of target audiences in the shortest possible span of time.

With the click of a few buttons, content spreads like wildfire across social media. Referral traffic is huge on social media, and content can be quickly disseminated to a high number of targeted folks.

Ensure that your content is aligned with your brand values and the preferences and interests of your target audience. According to consumer psychology, it takes around six to eight exposures for a person to make a decision about purchasing a product.

The use of social media gives that vital repeat exposure to consumers, constantly reminding them about your products and services. Thus, your sales funnel is considerably shortened.

9. *Positions You as an Industry Influencer* – Your influence keeps soaring as you gain new followers. The higher the number of followers on your brand's social media networks, the more credible, valuable, and dependable your brand will come across to potential customers. With a constant inflow of authoritative content, you can position yourself as a leading industry expert who knows what they're talking about.

People are more likely to purchase from experts who have proven their expertise with intelligent and thought-provoking insights over people who simply sell their products. Interaction with other big names in your industry also flatters your brand's profile and lends it more authenticity.

The more value you offer your readers, the more likely they are to return the favor by sharing your content and buying from you.

10. *Increases Conversion Opportunities* – Every post on social media awards you umpteen conversion opportunities. You have the chance of interacting with and targeting new, old, and potential customers with each shared video, image, blog or even a comment.

You never know which reaction may lead to customers visiting your site and ultimately buying something. That's the beauty of social media! Each interaction holds potential for a sale, without directly selling to your customers.

Even when customers do not make immediate purchases, they register the positive interaction for future buying decisions, eventually leading to a conversion.

If you have a large number of followers, the sales can be considerable even with low click-through rates (the percentage of visitors to a website page following a hyperlink text to a specific site, calculated by Total Clicks on the Ad/Total visitors to the page).

The number of potential customers turning into actual customers (conversion rate) is also high on social media due to the humanization factor.

People love brands that display a human element by sharing their behind-the-scenes-stories and engaging with customers. Social media is a platform that allows brands to be people and to have a personality. People like to do business with people, not faceless brands.

Audience building on social media can dramatically boost your existing traffic and, eventually, your conversion rates as well.

Chapter 2

# Facebook Marketing for Newbies

Currently, Facebook has an estimated base of 1.71 billion active users. Imagine the amount you are leaving behind on the table if you are not utilizing this powerful social media platform for promoting your brand.

Whether you use it as a free marketing or paid advertising tool, Facebook has the potential to help you reap rich dividends by giving you an incisively targeted customer base of people who are interested in your products and services.

According to a report published by Business2Community, 70% of marketing professionals use Facebook to attract new customers, and 47% of marketers name Facebook as the topmost influencer for purchase decisions. From a bare-bones college community, the social media giant has re-shaped the way we hold online interactions.

Facebook is primarily based on connections. It is all about building connections with old friends, colleagues, family, alumni networks, and of late it even helps build professional connections. Its sheer customization, visibility, and privacy settings give people a lot of choice and control over their interactions. You can choose to make certain posts visible only to specific people and choose who can view what on your profile.

Beyond individual profiles, even brand pages, groups, events pages, communities, and business pages have innumerable customization options for marketers to play around with.

**Setting Up a Presence on Facebook**

Planning and preparation is key before establishing a solid Facebook presence. Flesh out your brand personality before you set shop on Facebook.

This includes a logo, a clear communication style (for example, decide if you want a more humorous or officious style based on your brand values), recognizable branding with the use of design and color (Coca-Cola's Facebook page is a revelation where branding in concerned), a clear USP (unique selling point), and a thorough knowledge of your target audience.

These elements should also be consistent throughout all marketing and promotional channels, including other social media platforms, blogs, corporate websites, and so on.

Once you're through with the planning stage, set up a Facebook company page (can be groups or communities if you aren't keen on selling immediately but are more inclined toward building a solid community which can be sold to later). Here are some basic requirements once you set up your company page.

1. Get a professional designer to create professional, memorable, and meaningful logos, profile images and cover photos for your page. Make sure that the images are unique and congruent with your overall brand personality.

2. Ensure you have a professional, compelling, and articulate About Us section that best describes your company's background, products and services, and USP.

3. Mention important details such as the business's opening hours, email, contact number, physical address (if available), and other details your customers may want to know.

4. Have a few posts ready before you create your page. These may be curated content (content syndicated from other sites/blogs), images to gather reactions, appealing videos that can be widely shared, and insightful blogs posts.

5. Use high resolution images for describing your products and services along with pithy and interesting descriptions to go along with them. Keep your product and service descriptions brief, attention-grabbing, and informative.

6. Preferably, have a specific person or group of people manage your Facebook account to maintain a consistent voice and persona.

## Gain a Skyrocketing Following and Audience Engagement

Now that the basics are in place, here's where the real leg work begins. Gaining followers can be both easy and tricky depending on your understanding of your target audience. Here are some killer tips for helping to gain an avalanche of followers.

1. To begin with, invite existing people within your Facebook network, including family, friends, employees, business associates, etc. to like and follow your page. Once you have a decent following, it will be easier to enlist the support of outsiders.

People are naturally attracted to pages that have an established following, and tend to give pages with low or no following a miss. Hence, ensure that everybody from your network is invited and covered. An option to invite your friends to like a page is present on the page itself. Simply click on it and check friends whom you want to invite to the page by clicking their names.

2. Next, you can start following other big names in your industry, along with people and groups who you think may be interested in your products and services. Ensure that you don't mix up your personal profile and business page. In the

admin panel, located on top of your page, click on edit and select "Use Facebook as (your business name)."

Like all relevant groups, communities, and pages across your category. Leave messages, actively comment on their posts and share content to draw attention. Before you do all this, ensure that you read the rules of pages and groups to avoid being banned from them forever.

You may find the odd company that's hostile while interacting with competitors, but this is more of an exception than the rule. Most businesses on social media recognize the value of industry networking by building online connections.

3. One grave mistake most beginning Facebook marketers make is focusing solely on gaining likes over increasing engagement. Engaging followers with your posts is as crucial as expanding your follower base. Social signals based on increased page activity are more important than mere likes.

A higher follower base can obviously help you boost engagement, but simply concentrating on acquiring new followers while failing to engage existing ones is a surefire way to Facebook marketing disaster.

4. User engagement is hugely influenced by the timing and frequency of your posts. If your posts aren't garnering enough reactions and/or shares, ask yourself if you are posting when your target audience is actually available to respond to those posts. Focus on engaging your customers at particular times.

For Facebook, the best time to post is during noon. Morning and evening rush hour timings are also great from the engagement perspective. Studies have revealed an 18% greater engagement rate on Thursday and Friday.

Though there have been differing opinions, most experts agree that 1pm to 3pm is a good time for scheduling Facebook posts for higher engagement and click-through rates. Lunch breaks, rush hours, and post-dinner hours are tested to be a good time for audience involvement. You may have to consider time zones if you are targeting customers across different states and countries.

A Buddy Media study has revealed that pages which post about one to two posts a day enjoy 40% more user engagement than pages that post more than thrice a day. This clearly establishes that the social media audience seeks more quality than quantity.

5. One of the best tips for increasing your followers is an absolute no-brainer, yet you'd be surprised how many people actually overlook it. Check your successful and widely followed competitor pages to see what they are doing to draw audience. Some of the insights you gain using this method can be extremely revealing.

Since the nature of every business is different, there cannot be a standard set of ideas for engaging followers on Facebook. A strategy that can work miraculously for one business may be an absolute disaster for another. Find pages similar to yours doing a basic Facebook or Google searches and emulate their audience engagement strategies for gaining new followers.

6. Create original, valuable and attention-grabbing content. Post content that is useful or simply fun for your target audience. Make your blog posts detailed, grammatically correct, well-researched, and hugely impressive before sharing them on social media. People love to share information or posts that make them come across as smart among online social networks (referred to as social currency in Johan Berger's book Contagious, which discusses why things catch on).

If you create content that increases the "social currency" of your target audience within their circle of influence, they are more likely to share it. People love to flaunt the fact that they are up-to-date with information about things that affect them and their peers. Cash in on this syndrome by creating unique, focused, and compulsively readable content. Back your posts with professional and high resolution images that match the overall sentiment of the post.

To keep your credibility from shattering, check all content for grammatical errors and factual discrepancies. Do not share content originating from dubious sites. In short, don't do anything that will take away from your awesomeness. Pro tip: Infographics are one of the most widely shared content formats. Create comprehensive, industry-relevant and detailed infographics using infogr.am.

7. Check what's catching on like wildfire. Buzzsumo is a great place to check out what's going viral in your niche. Once you are aware of the topics received well by people, create posts centered on the same theme or idea.

For instance, if you run a travel business related page, you may come to realize that some of the most widely shared posts on Facebook according to Buzzsumo are those related to pet travel. There, now you have a bagful of content ideas that can be shared by a passionate pet traveling community. If you want higher engagement and shares, avoid hackneyed content and scour for new angles. People quickly lap up novelty.

8. Place a Facebook Page Plugin prominently on your blog or website to make it easy for readers to follow you on Facebook. Like buttons next to blog posts are great for sharing content but the page plugin will help increase the actual page likes and increase your following.

Promoting your Facebook page across different social networks such as LinkedIn or Twitter is also an astute move. People won't be pushed into taking action with a mere "Like Us On Facebook" button. You may have to divert your connections (followers) to conversations happening on your Facebook page.

9. Engage with similar pages within your industry. You can frequently leave behind thought-provoking, smart, and well-researched comments on other pages.

Responding intelligently or humorously to posts on other highly followed pages will make their followers sit up and take notice of your page. This not only helps you develop a rapport with other pages and build industry connection networks, but also boosts your page engagement. Ensure that you comment using your business page and not your personal profile.

Another little known insider tip is to tag similar pages in your posts. This way your post appears on the walls of other pages, thus sparking an interest among their founders and fans.

10. Always enable the similar page suggestions option in your settings. This is another lesser known yet highly effective trick for attracting lots of free likes for your page. When a user likes your competitor's page, Facebook automatically recommends your page to them under "similar page suggestions." All you need to do is enable your "similar page suggestions" option, which can be located in the page's settings.

11. Contests, freebies, and giveaways are great ways to get your audience to share posts on Facebook. Post monthly or weekly giveaways to entice people to share your post with their friends.

Contest and freebie posts spread rapidly, and can quickly help you skyrocket your following. You can ask people to like your page, comment on the thread, share the post on their wall, or tag their friends to qualify for the giveaway.

Don't make it too complicated and time-consuming. Liking the page and sharing should be the basic requirement. Get creative and come up with something that holds the interest of your target audience.

For example, if you deal in baby products, you could have a cutest baby contest by asking parents to like your page, post images of their baby in the comments section, and share your post. This way you are reaching hundreds of friends of every single parent who participates.

This is more cost effective than monumental advertising budgets, and insanely interesting! Keep coming up with creative contests and giveaways to increase audience participation and sharing.

Another great way to garner more likes is to offer your Facebook fans and followers exclusive insider discounts for liking your page. According to a Syncapse study, 42% of respondents admitted to liking pages for discounts and money-saver coupons.

12. Follow the 80-20 content rule when it comes to posting on Facebook. This means reserving 80% of your posts for informational and engaging content, while devoting only 20% to promotional content. This ratio will vary, depending on your business. On the whole, however, this is a good strategy to follow.

As discussed earlier, social media is not a platform for selling per se. It is more a channel for creating a build-up to the sale by forging strong connections with your audience.

13. Referencing your Facebook page in your blog posts is a great way to direct readers to your page. People don't simply like clicking on buttons that say "like us" or "follow us." They follow pages when there's something interesting in it for them.

If you've had a particularly interesting discussion on a Facebook post, go ahead and reference it by linking to the post from your blog. People who are reading your blog are already interested in your products or services, and will be more eager to check out discussions related to the blog post.

14. Create topical groups. Sometimes, consumers are wary of liking brand pages. It's not like they don't buy stuff, they are just tired of receiving marketing messages and seek more meaningful engagements. Get these folks involved with topical Facebook groups.

Create a group related to your industry that may interest your target audience. Say a group for mothers if you are into child care products or a group for car enthusiasts if you are a distributor of automobile parts.

Groups may not help your branding strategy as much as a proper business page, but you will most likely enjoy higher engagement. People like to participate in predominantly non-promotional groups that add more value to their life.

If you are looking to build relationships, trust, and connections over simply peddling your goods and services, groups may be a better bet. They may not have a uniform voice or tone, but they can be far more interesting and flexible than a regular business page.

15. Keep your Facebook posts short and appealing. Research conducted by Blitzlocal has suggested that shorter Facebook posts (100-120 characters) are likely to attract the highest audience engagement.

Users on the Internet have a limited attention span, with hundreds of businesses trying to capture interest. People do not spend more than few seconds to size up your post and decide if it's worth their while to get involved in your content.

Posts that are short, snappy, and out of the ordinary are likely to enjoy greater engagement than elaborate and verbose material. Asking short, direct, and thought-provoking questions is a great way to spark dialogues and get people to respond on Facebook.

16. Equip yourself with the image arsenal. A picture is worth more than a thousand words on Facebook. Images are a superb way to attract customers and build engagement. They help your posts stand out from uninspiring links and wordy status updates.

Clear, bright, and eye-catching images instantly increase the desirability of your products and services. They are also more digestible than long-winded textual posts for attention-starved users.

A ladies' fashion apparel brand, Leneys, uses the power of images brilliantly to engage their audience. They frequently post multiple images and ask followers to pick their favorite attire. A single such post garnered them more than 50 comments, 55 shares, and an impressive 52 likes.

Ensure that you don't steal photos by taking them from a Google image search. There are a lot of copyright laws related to images on the Internet and you could get into serious legal trouble if you use photographs and images without permission of the creators.

Instead, use images you create, buy images from stock photo sites, or use free images from sites such as Pixabay (read their terms and conditions carefully). You can also use images from Wiki Commons with proper attribution (read rules carefully as they vary from image to image).

17. Use "Call-to-Action" effectively for greater engagement. Calls to action are essentially psychological nudges which propel customers to respond. These may not necessarily be related to taking a purchase-related action, but simply ask your customers to respond in some way to what you've posted.

Taking the discussion above from how attention-depraved social media users are, let's make it easier for them to react by giving them specific details about how to respond.

What exactly do you want your followers to do? Comment on a post? Share or like it? Create posts that help them do exactly what you want them to do.

Take an example of Subway's Facebook page. They keep posting beautiful images and include a simple yet powerful "Call-to-Action" to get customers to react. One such post had an image of a beautiful beach along with a caption asking users to "like" the post if they wished to spend their Sunday on a beach. Now, it doesn't take a genius to figure out that most people would enjoy lazy weekend beach trips.

However, how many people actually think of getting their users engaged by asking them something so obvious? Very few. The post gathered more than 53,000 likes and over 400 shares. Not bad, right?

You have to guide people into doing what you want them to do without making it too apparent. Post things that your target audience is passionate about, or something that drives them.

18. Inject wit and humor into your posts. Everyone loves a good laugh in the midst of day-to-day stress (little wonder that those cat and dog dancing videos are so popular). Humor lends a more personal and informal tone to your interactions.

Though it may vary from business to business, virtually any type of business can inject humor into their posts to make them more fun and appealing.

People love the positive vibes of a feel good and humorous post, and these happy vibes are ultimately transmitted to your brand. They instantly associate your brand with positivity and cheer, thus rendering it more likeable.

Take the example of how Groupon converted a potentially embarrassing post into a downright hilarious affair, which was widely shared across various social media platforms as an epitome of social media expression. They posted an image of rather risqué looking banana holders. Users were obviously thrilled at the prospect of trolling them, little knowing what was in store for them.

Rather than replying caustically to the trolls, their bunch of social media superstars came up with insanely funny comebacks for each comment. For instance, Jane's comment, "What if our bananas are too big?" was met with, "Don't exaggerate." It made for a fun read and you bet all their banana holders were completely sold out.

18. Crowdsource for queries. Another whopper of a tip for increasing your engagement is to allow other users to answer questions rather than answering it yourself. Natural Parenting Tips has mastered this strategy rather well. As the name suggests, it is a page that focuses on offering parenting advice and tips.

Each day they post their fans' questions, while inviting others to help. The idea is to gather suggestions, advice, and tips from their parent fan base. This not just helps the fan who has asked the question, but also other parents. Give this tip a try and witness how active your fans can be when it comes to offering advice about something they can closely relate to.

Chapter 3

# The Beginner's Guide to Pinterest

Social media's image-conscious player, Pinterest, has got everyone raving, and with good reason. The site is nothing but a virtual counterpart of pin boards that we've all used for collecting our favorite images and write-ups.

Pinterest has lent a pretty glamorous sheen to a simple, everyday concept. It invites users to create "pinboards" for selecting and sharing images, videos, and write-ups related to their interests. With close to 100 million unique users, the site is slated to grow phenomenally in coming years. It is currently the third largest social media site, just after Facebook and Twitter.

In average minutes spent per month on the site, Pinterest is second only to Facebook. Pinterest users spend an average of 89 minutes per month creating and browsing pinboards, while Facebook records an average of 405 minutes per user each month. Impressive? You bet.

However, some businesses still fail to capitalize on the unique and interesting features of Pinterest simply because they don't realize how it can add value to their business. Here's everything you need to know to get started.

**Let's understand some basic Pinterest lingo first**
*Pin* – This is the visual counterpart of a Facebook or Twitter post. These posts are in the form of images that are added from various blogs and websites by clicking on the 'Pin It' button. You can also upload your own images from a computer or other devices. Every pin added by clicking on the "Pin It" option can take users back (links to) to the site/blog it originated from.

*Board* – This is a compilation of pins focused on a single theme or topic. For instance - kitchen décor, cocktails, DIY crafts for kids, and other similar topics. Think of it as the virtual version of image boards.

*Following* – "Following All" allows of the pins and boards of a particular user to show up on your timeline. If you are interested in what someone pins, all you have to do is follow their account. Followers, on the other hand, are those who follow your pins or a specific board.

*Repin* – A Repin is simply adding pins that you find by browsing through Pinterest to your board. The user who originally pinned the image gets attributed each time their image is repinned. Repins keep the link to the original blog or website intact, irrespective of the repinned numbers.

## The Pinterest Home Page

The home page is the first thing you'll come across after you register and sign in. This page has a main board, which is a selection of all followed pins. It is similar to a Twitter or Facebook feed or stream. The main board is called the Following Board. It features all the pins from the various boards you follow, including the number of likes, comments, and repins the original pin has garnered.

On the homepage's upper left corner, there are updates about Recent Activity that shows if anyone started following the boards and pins you created, liked your pin, or repinned a pin.

Other than the pins you are already following, the homepage allows you to filter other pins. You can pick categories that you want to see. For instance, if you select "Travel," you'll be able to see the pins and boards which are tagged with a matching description.

The "All" section is a single board that pulls in every user's images and pins. "Popular Pins," on the other hand, features pins that have garnered the highest number of likes, comments, or repins. These can be seen as the trending Pinterest pins.

The home page also features a unique "Gifts" section. It's pretty similar to the "Everything" option, with the exception that all pins added here come with a price tag.

Any pin with an attached price is by default added to the "Gifts" section (for example, a $10-30 price range). All you have to do to include a pin in "Gifts" is add a price in the description. If you are looking for a specific Pinterest account, use the search bar located in the top-left corner.

**How to Create a Pinterest Board**
*Step 1*: For creating a Board, go to Add on the top right corner of the site and click on Create Board.

*Step 2*: Give the board a title and pick a relevant category. Picking the right category is crucial as it will help users locate your boards easily while scouring for Interests.

**How to Add and Upload a Pin**
*Step 1*: Click Add and select the Add a Pin option.

*Step 2*: Paste the URL to be posted and click on Find Images.

*Step 3*: Pinterest will launch a search for all images within the article. Ensure the post has a relevant title. Click Pin It and share the pin on the appropriate board within the drop down menu options.

For uploading pins, you simply click on Upload a Pin by going to Add in the top right corner of your page.

**Killer Pinterest Marketing Tips for Beginners**

*Get Creative* – The entire medium of Pinterest in based on creativity and visual appeal. The several businesses that view Pinterest as a predominantly crafts and cooking platform can take a cue from GE. The nature of their services isn't something you'd immediately associate with Pinterest.

However, they frequently update their feed with superbly inspiring boards dedicated to kitchen ideas, geeky gifts, and more. With some ingenuity, virtually any business can harness the power of this visually captivating social network.

*Include Relevant Details* – Sometimes people are all set to buy the pinned items they come across. Simply add a price to your pinned or repinned images to make it easier for users. Pins with prices attached are said to gather 36% more likes than those without price tags.

However, ensure that you aren't just selling. Make your boards a nice combination of utility, ideas, and sales. Most users are browsing for ideas and inspiration, which should be given to them if you want to attract more followers.

*Humanize Your Brand Visually* – You may want to check Ben and Jerry's as an exemplary example of how they've captured the behind-the-scenes human aspect of their brand by sharing details about the brand's history, the stories of their employees, and more.

The jam-packed marketing world could do with breath of fresh air in the form of fuzzy, feel-good human stories. This adds a more personal touch to your marketing campaign and ensures greater brand loyalty.

*Repin the Most Successful Pins* – One of the best strategies that businesses often fail to capitalize on is repining pins that are hot and gathering plenty of attention on Pinterest. Repinning the most popular pins will increase repins.

These may not promote your blog post or website, but your followers will get into the habit of visiting your profile and repinning pins selected by you. Once they view your profile, it won't take them much time to start repinning your original pins, which can give you considerable exposure.

*Pin Blog Posts* ¬– Relationships on social media are built by value. Offers your visitors value, and they are likely to stick with you. Help them get that value from you by simplifying the actions you want them to perform. Trust is built only when people consistently discover the value you offer.

Pin your blog posts by scheduling them for the most optimal times. For Pinterest, the best time to pin something is 2pm, 4pm and 8pm. Include a short summary for the blog post along with appropriate keywords (to make it easily traceable in search engine results).

*Go Beyond the Niche* ¬ - Pinterest is a brilliant platform to showcase your hobbies and interests, along with a professional profile. Go beyond your professional avatar to pin a more personal picture for your followers. Everyone likes to see the "real person" behind a professional persona. Include your hobbies, personality traits, and interests in the bio. Engage in conversation with people who share similar interests.

You will have a field day discussing felines with fellow cat fans if you mention "cat lover" in your Pinterest bio. Shared interests create a greater sense of belonging, thereby increasing the chances of users eventually buying from you.

*Participate in Group Boards* – Imagine if you could promote something to thousands of people without too much effort. Group boards are a boon for people who want to gain a following by contributing. The reason why group boards are so insanely popular on Pinterest is because when a user participates in group board, the board automatically appears on their profile.

When new followers click the "Follow All" option, the user follows each board within a profile, including group boards. People want a higher number of users within a group, since higher contributions means more engagement and greater exposure. Therefore, getting accepted into groups can be quite easy. Once in a group, your profile is easily accessible to the thousands of followers within that group. Works both ways, right?

You profile ends up looking more attractive with a nice assortment of updated boards. When you pin on a high activity group board, you are tapping into a large audience base and getting more followers in the bargain.

*Create Optimized Descriptions* – Pinterest gives you a maximum of 500 characters, though you shouldn't make your posts that long. Users on Pinterest prefer pithy and snappy posts, where images do all the talking. Keep the description a little over a Tweet (200-250 characters should be your hot spot) for eliciting maximum repins.

Ensure that your description is optimized with appropriate keywords, a couple of hashtags, and most importantly, a Call-to-Action such as clicking on the image to visit the blog or article.

Hashtags and keywords are essential if you want users to easily locate your pins using the platform's search engine. This leads to better exposure for your brand. And who doesn't need more spotlight?

*Bring the Influencer's Leverage* – Use the power of influencers to build awareness about your brand by collaborating with them on busy group boards.

This won't just make you profile more flattering, it will also make you come across as someone who is constantly engaging with followers and contributing to the board. A double whammy!

*Images Without Faces* – Strange as this may seem, images without faces are likely to gather 23% more repins than those with faces. It seems that visually driven users on Pinterest do not want to see pretty faces, but inspiring ideas. Focus on pinning non-people focused images.

Creative ideas, resourcefulness, novelty and inspiration are the key. People use Pinterest as a tool for generating and collecting ideas. Make your pins more idea-centric.

*Avoid Spamming Boards with Self-Promotion* – Though this may seem like a lovely platform for promoting small and mid-sized enterprises, avoid spamming boards with excessive self-promotion. Pinterest users frown upon too much self-endorsement and are more accepting of people who add value by contributing to the community. It is considered good Pinterest etiquette to link and connect by sharing images that truly inspire your brand's work rather than blatantly selling your products and services.

What things and ideas shape your company's vision? Where do you draw your inspiration from? What is the story behind your brand? Sharing all this will help you build more meaningful connections on Pinterest. Self-promotion, if anything, should be more creative and subtle.

Use the Pinterest platform for building trust, forging a strong community of like-minded folks, and grabbing attention. The platform is more of a community than a place for doing business. People here appreciate each other's recommendations and suggestions. Research has revealed that Pinterest users spend more per referral on Pinterest than any social network.

While shoppers from Facebook average at spending $60-80, Pinterest sits comfortably at $140-180). This means people make more high-end purchases based on recommendations on Pinterest. This should give you enough motivation to create Pinterest promotion campaigns that work!

*Tutorials are the Way to Go* – Since sharing ideas and helping people is the bedrock of Pinterest, try to help your customers rather than pushing products or services on them. The click-through rate for guides and tutorial-based pins is a staggering 42% more than regular pins; people click on useful things that make their lives easier.

Rather than creating pins about your products or services, why not show users how to use these products or services optimally? If you run an online organic grocery store, rather than promoting the fresh greens, why not share pins of delicious and healthy organic breakfast recipes or inventive organic smoothies? Get the drift? It is all about giving before you take.

*Use Warm and Bright Colors* – Other than the obvious guideline of using clear and high-quality images, keep in mind that bright and warm toned pictures get twice as many repins than cool colors like blue and green. Try and stick to images bearing flaming colors such as orange, deep red, brown, burgundy, etc. to garner more repins.

*Little Known Tools* – Like most social media platforms, Pinterest has its own set of valuable tools that can be used to optimize your networking and/or promotional campaigns. Use Viraltag for scheduling pins, while Curalate can help you with audience insights (web traffic stats, engagement levels, and people's response to pins). Pinalerts are great for getting instant notifications about engagement.

Chapter 4

# Twitter Marketing for Beginners

Your business needs Twitter. Period. It can be overwhelming for new users with its character limit, frenzied feed, and multiple features. However, being one of the most active and popular social media platforms, there's no way you can ignore it.

A solid Twitter presence gives you access to a huge database of potential customers who can be engaged with a single Tweet. The microblogging giant currently has 313 million active monthly users, and more than 400 million tweets are sent per day. You're leaving a lot of money on the table if you're not harnessing the potential of this versatile and dynamic social media network.

**Establish a Clear Strategy**
Have a clear social media plan in place before starting on Twitter. What are you aiming to achieve through a Twitter

presence? Higher engagement? Building a corporate brand? Better customer service? Networking with other industry professionals? Or all of it? Your overall strategy should be congruent with your marketing or business goals.

**Create an Impactful Profile and Cover Image**
Your Twitter profile should ideally be your corporate logo or a professional image of yourself. It should be uniform with other social networks, where you already have or are trying to establish a social presence. Get a graphic designer to create a killer logo that packs plenty of punch.

The cover image again should be high-resolution, attention-grabbing, and catchy. It should complement your profile picture and go with the overall brand persona or the "voice" of your brand. Ensure you add your business website (experts recommend using a dedicated Twitter landing page and including it in the profile URL section for a more personal and relevant user experience) and a compelling Call-to-Action. You can keep changing the Call-to-Action depending on the latest trends, products and services, or seasons.

**Get Noticed**
Your aim on Twitter from day one should be to get noticed for your awesomeness. One of the best ways to do this is by using the hashtag (more on that later). Ensure your hashtags are relevant, snappy, memorable, and interesting. Restrict the number of hashtags to about 2-3 per post, else you risk losing engagement.

Another nice tip to up your desirability quotient is re-tweeting great stuff related to your industry. Include your own attention-grabbing comment about why you think it's worth sharing. Participating and hosting Twitter chat parties is a great way to contribute and engage with a highly focused audience.

**Build a Strong Following**
One of the best ways to build a following on Twitter is by citing other Twitter influencers in your industry. This will show up on their feed, they will be notified and most likely openly express their gratitude, thus giving you an opportunity to be followed by thousands of their targeted followers.

Stay in tune with the latest trends to create events, hashtags, and topical tweets about them. These can cater to a general as well as niche audience. When you quote tweets of other users or influencers in your blog, inform them. They may share the post with their followers, since well everyone loves to be recognized as an expert. And yippee, you get increased exposure!

**Remove Spammy Accounts**
Keep evaluating your Twitter following periodically for blocking spammy and dubious accounts. This frequent spring cleaning will ensure you have real, solid, and engaged users rather than a bunch of spammers who can harm your Twitter authority.

Everyone wants to enjoy a high following, but allowing spammy accounts to follow you just to flaunt big numbers is a definite highway to Twitter hell. Having a small group of loyal and genuine followers is better than being followed by thousands of fake and inactive users who can hurt your account.

**Voice and Branding**

The nature of Twitter is such that you have only 140 characters to make or break your reputation, which means each word matters. Your company's unique voice will trickle into each interaction. So, what should be the ideal tone of your brand? How should you react to customer complaints and conflict?

Should you maintain a more humorous or serious stance through your interactions? You need to decide this beforehand in order to keep interactions in line with your overall brand values and corporate goals. Interactions shouldn't be based on whether you've got your cup of evening coffee, or your mood.

There should be absolute consistency and uniformity in your tone. Over time, this consistency will help followers know what to expect from your interactions with them, which will invariably shape your brand identity or image. It will come to define your fundamental brand persona.

**Be Interesting and Addictive**

Twitter isn't the medium to be loquacious, though you need to constantly reinforce your presence through interesting and compulsively readable tweets. Let them offer value over being overtly promotional. Offering 50% discount on a newly launched product may seem like an attractive proposition, but followers will soon get tired of seeing your company with the same sales lens. Bring about a shift from marketing to revealing your personal brand by adding value.

Fast food giant Taco Bell has an innately snarky Twitter persona, which is consistently evident in their engaging, humorous, and irreverent tweets. Taco Bell has mastered the art of being bang on their brand identity, and it works wonderfully for them. Look at their content strategy and customer engagement – simply brilliant!

**Quick Response Is the Key**
What is it they say about the early bird getting the worm? Well, it can't be any truer than on Twitter. It is essential to respond to customer queries and complaints as quickly as possible. Customer service needs rapid attention owing to the speedy pace and condensed nature of the network.

If you take long to reply to a critical tweet, other followers may amplify the single voice, and it may spiral beyond control. That being said, don't just Twitter for damage control or to answer queries. Keep popping up to greet your followers and share positive things. Also, acknowledge the appreciation that comes your brand's way.

## Scheduling Twitter Updates

You or your social media manager may not always be available at the time you actually want your tweet to be released. Scheduling updates is a great way to publish tweets when your follower community is active. Obviously, posts related to breaking news such as global disasters or local tragedies will need quick, on-the-spot updates; however, for other more strategically planned updates, you can organize yourself and make your work much easier by scheduling updates.

## Replying on Twitter

People generally use the @username to reply to someone on Twitter. A sample of this would look something like:

@username Thank you. I am glad you loved our food!

This will make your Tweet visible only to your followers and the followers of the person/business you've tagged. If you want more people to be able to view the post, use a period or another marker before the @ sign on the username.

## Retweeting

Retweeting is simply sharing someone else's tweet with your followers. You simply re-share with your followers what someone else has shared with their followers.

To manually retweet something, you open a separate tweet box and paste the tweet into it. Add RT and the author or company's handle (@username) to display that you've shared someone else's tweet. You can also automatically retweet by clicking on the two arrow options placed between "reply" and "like" below every tweet.

Adding a comment of your own at the top of the retweet is a great way to add your own voice to it.

Educate, entertain, and illuminate your audience with your retweets. In short, add the wow factor or make them smile. You can find interesting and retweetable trivia even for the most officious brands.

For instance, lawyers or law firms can take a break from heavy topics and bring some laughs by retweeting trivia related to the most hilariously outdated laws. Add clever industry related one-liners or tweet something humorous about a current event or trend. Always retain the original source of the tweet if you're retweeting.

Retweeting is good Twitter etiquette because you aren't simply stealing someone else's content, but giving them due credit for it. However, retweet sparingly by choosing only those tweets that stand out or should not be missed by your target audience. Avoid being offensive or controversial.

Create memorable and unique tweets of your own that others would love to retweet. This boosts your brand authority and social signals.

**Hashtags**

Hashtags present your message to a larger audience. People who may not be following you can follow updates posted by you based on hashtags. Hashtags are like condensed signposts that interestingly capture the essence of your message in a few characters.

The social media phenomenon of hashtagging became so successful and prevalent that it found itself in the Oxford dictionary.

Rather than creating hashtags that promote your business, build hashtags around value propositions and human elements.

Hashtags can range from profoundly meaningful to downright irreverent, as long as it grabs the attention of your target audience. You wouldn't expect something as banal as toilet paper to catch like wildfire on social media, yet Charmin's insanely clever #TweetFromTheSeat did just that. Research indicated that a lot of people access social media from the comfortable confines of their toilet seat. Charmin's creative brains sprang into action and decided to create a campaign where followers were asked to post selfies while being seated on the 'big throne.' Charmin's hashtag campaign became a huge success.

If you follow a few rules when it comes to hashtags, you aren't very far from Twitter glory.

One of the worst things to do is create hashtags that bear the name of your brand. Nope, hashtags aren't meant to do that. That's blatant ego massaging. Keep hashtags compatible with the tone, values and vision of your brand. Dove's #speakbeautiful campaign captured the spirit of the brand's focus on natural, innocent, and real beauty rather well.

Your hashtags should reveal what your brand fervently represents rather than the brand itself. Humanize it. Add fun. Make it personal. People love to participate in discussions on hashtags they can relate to. Your hashtags should be actionable and instantly catchy. Hashtagging is all about reinforcing your brand's personality and not about getting people to worship your brand (though with great hashtags, eventually they will).

Do not make your hashtags complex or difficult to remember. Use desirable, fun, in-vogue words that people can easily remember and relate to. Make it rhyme. Use clever wordplay or puns. Hashtags should make it easy for users to search for your posts. Humanize these tags by associating them with a powerful emotion. Make A Wish's #sffbatkid is a brilliant example of how the foundation promoted a documentary of one of their members to evoke powerful emotions among followers.

When someone retweets your post, acknowledge it by thanking them for it. This way, you are not just establishing yourself as the original author of the tweet but also coming across as more approachable to their followers.

**Twitter Parties**

Twitter parties allow you to thank your followers and build a loyal community by hosting engaging virtual get-togethers. You may have to determine how to weave this strategy into the nature of your business, since it may not be relevant for all enterprises.

Twitter events are a great way to gather more followers, engage existing followers, and generally create buzz about your products and services without actually selling them. Typically, these Twitter events last between 12 and 24 hours. Hosting them monthly is a great idea to keep the interest factor alive.

Create a catchy and memorable hashtag specifically for the event. You can add videos of previous Twitter parties to let new followers know what's in store for them or spread the word about your new products and services without selling. Trust that people who have fun will act as the ultimate evangelists for your brand.

**Step-by-Step Guide on How to Host a Twitter Party or Event**

Before you start hosting a Twitter party, zero in on a theme related to your brand. Know exactly what drives your target audience and what they'd really be interested in. Invoking their passions and interests is a great way to get them involved. What's you core objective of hosting the event? Do you want to gain new followers or simply awaken the slumbering folks? Are you testing the market for a potential product, or do you want to create a strong buzz about a newly launched product or service? Working out a clear objective will help you formulate a strategy that's in line with your basic goals.

1. *Pick a Topic* – You need a central theme, topic, or idea that's closely related to your brand for your Twitter party. It should be something powerful that immediately stirs engagement. Contests and training sessions are a great way to give back to your audience.

For instance, if you are into beauty or make-up products or grooming services, you can gather a group of raving make-up lovers for a #funfridaymakeupbash where you and all followers share their favorite make-up secrets over interesting conversation and discussions.

2. *Create a Hashtag* – Use all the points and expert tips mentioned above under the hashtags section to create a unique, memorable, and attention-grabbing hashtag for the event. Keep it simple and relevant.

3. *Schedule the Event* - You will want to schedule your event at a time when your followers are most active on Twitter. This can vary from topic to topic. However, generally speaking 1pm to 4pm Eastern Time is a good time to ensure maximum participation.

4. *Promote the Event* – You have to spread the message about your upcoming event a few days before the event. Inform your followers beforehand to mark the date and keep themselves free during the event hours. This will also allow them to distribute the message among their followers, thus ensuring a sizeable participation for the event.

5. *Plan Your Tweets in Advance* – Of course, wit, spontaneity, and relevant responses are the hallmark of a successful social media event, but you also need to have a ready bank of pre-planned tweets to stir the discussion and conversation in the direction you want. Otherwise, the event might end up being a free-for-all, where everyone other than you is promoting themselves and their products and services.

You need to tactfully control and divert the chat in the direction you want, while also allowing it to flow naturally. Use Buffer or Hootsuite to schedule your Tweets in advance.

6. *Send Out Constant Reminders* – You need to keep reminding your followers about the upcoming event without annoying them. Reminder posts are a good way to put the event on top of their head if they've forgotten about it but are enthusiastic about being a part of it.

7. *Assign Tasks* – You may need more than one person to carry out specific tasks related to the event. For instance, one moderator can monitor tweets, while the other can pick contest winners or respond to participants.

8. *Host the Party* – You need to be extremely attentive, keen, and focused throughout the party. However, that shouldn't stop you from enjoying it. Launch Hootsuite or Buffer to be kept in the loop about the latest social media buzz related to your party.

9. *Send Prizes* – Do not forget to quickly send out the prizes once the event concludes. Ask winners to notify you about their email address through direct messaging. You can add their email address to your mail list for future updates and newsletters.

10. *Obtain Feedback* – What's the point in having a party when you don't get to know what everyone thought about it? Even for regular parties, don't we want to know if our guests had a great time? Create a survey or send out an email to obtain feedback about the event. Analyze what you did well and what you can do better, and incorporate the necessary suggestions in your next virtual bash.

Chapter 5

# Instagramming for Social Media Success

Instagram features more than 400 million users with over 70 million images shared every day. More than 90% of Instagram users are under 35 years of age. This should be enough reason for you to make it a component of your social media mix. Here's a complete beginner's guide for Instagram marketing success.

*Download the Instagram App* – Download the Instagram app from the app store. You will have to sync the app with your iOS device if you are downloading from iTunes.

*Create an Account* – Click on "Sign Up" at the bottom of the app screen to enter all details such as your username, password, email, and, optionally, your phone number. You can add a brief and interesting personal or company introduction under the "About" section. Ensure that you include your business or personal website.

*Follow Friends* – You can either import contacts and located friends from your existing contact list or manually search for friends using their usernames. Following people allows you to view their updates on your feed. Just like with Twitter, you can follow people who you don't personally know such as celebrities and international figures.

Click "Next" once you are done. Instagram will suggest some users based on the users you are already following. You can follow these suggestions by clicking "Follow" adjacent to their usernames.

*The New Instagram Direct Update* – The recent Instagram update allows users to choose who they want to share their pictures with. Sometimes, you may not want to share every image with all your followers. This lets you customize settings about who gets to see what about your public feed.

*Scrolling and Discovering Photos* – Tap on the house-like icon on the left bottom toolbar. You can now scroll through all new posts of users you follow. There's a Discovery tab represented by a magnifying glass on top of the page. You can search for hashtagged posts and users with the Discovery tag by typing into the search bar.

*Viewing Updates* – When someone performs any activity related to your updates, such as commenting on an image, following you, tagging you, or more, you are notified in the "News" tab. You can display your interest in pictures by pressing the heart-shaped icon under the photo ("liking" the photo). For commenting on an image, simply click on the bubble icon and leave your comment.

*Adding Photographs on Instagram* – Click on the "Share" tab to select pictures from your device's image gallery. If you want to take a new photo and instantly upload it on Instagram, click the "Share" button followed by the camera icon. Click Next once you are done. Instagram doesn't have many editing options except for the standard rotation, adding frames, creating blurring photo effects, brightening photos and other similar features. Filters are quite popular with Instagram users. Scroll through the filters at the bottom of the image to pick the one that best suits your photograph.

*Adding a Description for the Image* – Enter a description under the "What" field. Adding a short description along with a couple of hashtags will make your post more searchable for users. A location can be added by selecting the "Where" option.

Chapter 6

# The Top 14 Instagram Marketing Secrets

1. *Partner With a Worthy Cause Compatible With Your Brand* – Collaborating with noble causes that are congruent with your brand values is a brilliant way to build a community on Instagram. Take SweetGreen, for instance. They are a lunch spot known for their organic and directly-from-farmers sourced ingredients. They've entered into a seamless partnership with FoodCorps that espouses healthy eating choices among children.

SweetGreen posted an image of a little girl digging into a bowl of fresh vegetables, which beautifully aligned with the values of both organizations. It was a well drafted post that successfully raised awareness about healthy eating choices, demonstrated the meaningful partnership between the two brands, and reinforced what SweetGreen stands for. Align your company's or website's values with customers.

2. *Share Your Brand Story* – Few things tug at people's heartstrings like a company story shared personably and compellingly. Use cool, interesting and meaningful images to present your company's fundamental values.

Make top executives appear approachable and human by posting quirky, funny, and interesting posts about them on Instagram. For instance, what are they most likely to do when they aren't working, or something really whacky and fun which people just wouldn't expect from them.

3. *Photo Captions and Contests* – A super way to increase engagement on Instragram is by sharing images of your products/service/niche or something related to your brand, and asking followers to have a blast captioning those images.

Pro tip: Try and hold a photo captioning contest, where you can encourage followers to participate by giving out cool prizes.

4. *Hashtagging Contests* – Hashtagging contests are the newest rage on Instagram. They are a fun and personalized to get users involved in content creation. Ask followers to upload photographs with your unique hashtag. They can then collectively vote for a winner.
Jorg Gory Gray created a nice hashtag contest. They asked visitors to share a photograph with a Jorg Gory Gray

timepiece using the #jorgstyle hashtag. Winners were given a free Jorg Gory Gray watch. Great way to build a fun and loyal following? You bet.

5. *Use hashtags* – Hashtags are an important part of Instagram and one of the best ways to wow followers. Connect with your audience by including a couple of unique, meaningful, and interesting hashtags. Don't overdo it or you'll come across as desperate.

Connect using the right emotions and values that are most likely to strike a chord with your target audience.

Make different hashtags for different campaigns to make it easier for you and your followers to keep track of multiple campaigns.

6. *Give Your Followers Some Fame* – Making your followers famous by sharing their photographs on Instagram is a great way to show them some much needed appreciation and win their hearts. Starbucks (which is one of the top three Instagram brands) successfully uses this strategy.

They often give a shout out for to their fans by including the a fan's image with Starbucks's most iconic products. The warm fuzzies feelings are further boosted when they use these images as fun Facebook covers.
Do the fans love it and come back for more? You bet. It is always good to seek permission from your fans before sharing their photographs.

Mention your followers with @username whenever you can, especially when they post pictures with your products. This is a great way to express gratitude and increase your involvement with your audience. Coke does this frequently. They often mention customers who win Instagram photo contests, making them feel super special and fuzzyvalued.

Since Instagram gives now offers you the option of directly embedding images from the network onto your site/blogwebsite or blog, use your customer's' images on your blog, too, to make them feel a part of your brand's loyal community.

7. *Showcase Your Products/Services Creatively* – Be hip, cool, and creative on Instagram. Pilot Pen USA is a superb example of how virtually any company can make it big on Instagram, and not just the ones selling clothes, cakes, and crafts.

Coming back to Pilot Pens, yYou may wonder how a company selling something as boring and uninspiring as pens comes up with attractive Instagram posts.

Well, creative thinking is the only secret sauce here. They post regular photographs of hand created notes using their pens?! And expectedly, their fans love the personal touch and relevance.

8. *Partner With with Other Brands* – Whether you are a one-man blog business or a mid-sized local business, there's always a scope way to forge meaningful relationships with other brands.

Partner up with other similar brands and get them to feature your products, while you post theirs on your Instagram feed. For instance, if you run a local cake shop or jewelry shop, you can get a popular wedding planner to feature your products on their feed, while you recommend their services to your followers. A sure-shot win-win.

9. *Have a Clear Branding Strategy* – Your brand is unique in its personality and in the way it sees the world. Connect your followers with the unique vibe of your brand. Build a link between your business (brand) and your Instagram tribe in a consistent and compellingly visual manner. Get your followers to adore your brand for its awesomeness.

10. *The Infallible Ask Technique* – One of the best ways to engage customers on Instagram (or most social media networks for that matter) is to simply ask. Don't assume oOnce you build an attractive page with a super line up of images, don't assume, that people will swarm like bees and create a buzz about your products/servicesto it on their own.

QQuestions are invitations for discussions and conversations. They may open up many new avenues which you may might not have thought about earlier.

Ask your fans relevant and interesting questions related to your products/ and services. Solicit opinion about a new product. Ask followers for tips or advice related to your industry. Create a unique hashtag and ask customers to share their experiences about your products or services.

For instance, if you run a service related to toddlers such as day care, a toy store, or something similar, you can ask parents to post pictures of their children with a unique hashtag and their number one toddler parenting tip. In this example, parents want to feel a part of a community and establish fruitful relationships with people who are in the same situation as they are. You create that community by being relevant to their needs, building connections, and giving them value.

11. *Build Story Arcs* – Well you've seen people sharing a bunch of attractive yet unrelated pictures together and garnering plenty of attention. Why not create stories out of these images by building a sequence around them? Think of creative story arcs, where each image can be used to take the story ahead. Images can also be posted to present progressions over a period of time. People love stories and actionable images that tell interesting stories.

12. *Experiment Withwith Your Product Images* – Think of new and interesting ways to showcase your products/ and services to your target audience. Use different settings and backgrounds to pique the curiosity of your followers. Create these images especially for Instagram and do not share them

on any other social media platform to maintain exclusivity. Creative photography and innovative product shoots add more punch to your profile. There are innumerable ways to do this even with standard products.

For example, salons and spas can post images of exquisite nail art with elegant hand postures or holding objects that complement the color scheme of the nail art. Visually dazzling? You bet. Pose with a violin or guitar to showcase nail art more creatively and unexpectedly.

If you run a beauty blog or beauty store or sell cosmetics, create a collage of various women wearing the same red lipstick to showcase how the shade can flatter different skin tones.

On a visually action-packed and dynamic platform like Instagram, visitors will soon lose interest if you simply keep posting dull and unexciting images of your products/ and services. You need to pump action into them to transform even the blandest products into Instagram superheroes.

13. *Use Videos* – Instagram has a godsent great feature (pardon the exaggeration) that allows users to record tiny video clips going up to 15 seconds. This opens up a whole new way to connect with your audience.

Use the feature to create stellar behind-the-scenes videos for your brand or tell a story about your employees or the company founder for that matter. Use its Instagram's filters innovatively to create stunning animations. You can create several videos and then splice them into something extraordinary.

14. *Avoid Negativity* – This should be self-evident, but given the conversations that happen on Instagram every day, it doesn't appear to be so. Be polite, civil, and professional in your interactions. There's no need to get sucked into dirt if one of the trolls is having a field day on your post. Rather than stopping stooping to their level, simply block them to retain your positivity and sanity.

Keep in mind that not everyone you follow will posts things that you agree with. This isn't reason enough to get agitated and spew venom on a social platform. Again, you can simply unfollow such folks rather than get into a senseless battle of wits.

When others behave badly, it is indeed a superb opportunity to showcase your grace and poise. Be tactful, and courteous, and avoid negative confrontations.

Chapter 7

# Cracking the LinkedIn Code

Often treated as the more officious and decorous social media step-child, LinkedIn remained staggeringly untapped for long. Until recently, people did not wise up to its marketing and promotional benefits. From a mere job and resume site, it has now become a powerful platform for forging professional connections and networks.

With over 450 million users, the business networking giant is slated to grow at a monumental pace in coming years.

It is a professional networking media all right. However, that's exactly why it is such a solid and dependable marketing platform. If you know the little known tricks and pro tips, there's nothing stopping you from creating a strong brand using LinkedIn. Here's everything you want to know about this social media superpower.

**Customize Your Profile URL**

Instead of having a profile URL with a zillion numbers on it, customize it by going to the profile URL option located in the right-hand corner. Your public profile will appear saner and more professional such as http:www.linkedin.com/JohnSmith.

**Add a Background Personal Profile Photo**

In 2104, LinkedIn finally opened itself up to the cover photo social media phenomenon. This adds a bit more persona and character to your profile. Ensure you pick a profile that's in tandem with the professional social media tone of LinkedIn.

Add a background profile photo by clicking on Profile > Edit Profile (LinkedIn's upper navigation bar) > Add a Background Photo. You can modify an existing background photo by clicking on it and selecting the Edit Background option.

Your cover photo, according to LinkedIn specifications, must be a PNG, GIF or JPG file only (under 8 MG). The ideal resolution is 1400 x 425 pixels.

**Add the LinkedIn Badge**

Another unique and professionally befitting feature that LinkedIn has is the Profile Badge. Expand your professional connections by displaying this badge (there are many options to pick from) on your blog or website. It links directly to your LinkedIn profile.

**Display Work Samples**

Well, people are searching you on LinkedIn because they want to see your professional work before associating with you.

Not many know that LinkedIn offers the feature of adding tons of media including videos, graphics, documents, and presentations under the Experience, Summary and Education sections of your profile. Use them to showcase your brilliance.

Add projects and portfolios. Try to add a variety of samples to give potential clients a glimpse of your versatility.

**Recommend People**
LinkedIn focuses heavily of building business networks and recommending people professionally.

When you recommend people, you find them returning the favor by treating your brand more positively. You not just feel good about endorsing a worthy product and service, but you also attract goodwill for your own brand, lasting professional partnerships, and greater participation.

**Join Groups**
Groups are one of the best ways to draw traffic to your profile. Join as many relevant groups as you can and contribute regularly. Active participation is key when it comes to being a seamless part of a thriving professional community.

Share interesting and industry-relevant content, initiate thought-provoking discussions, and contribute to existing conversations. This establishes the credibility of your brand, while giving you access to a whole new world of professional connections.

Lasting client-brand relationships and brand promotion is what you should aim for while creating formidable groups. However, don't sell yourself too hard. Focus instead on selling your brilliance and knowledge by creating and sharing top notch content.

When people become a part of specific groups, it shows up on their profile, thus triggering the curiosity of their connections. Additionally, group members can view each other's profiles without actually being connected.

The best way to reach out to potential customers and associates via LinkedIn is by joining as many groups as possible.

When two people are part of one group, the need to be a first degree connection (direct connection of a person rather than the connection of a connection) is eliminated for having a direct conversation.

If you've been on LinkedIn for a month and a member of the group for a minimum of 4 days, LinkedIn lets you send 15 one-on-one messages free to all group members for every group you are a part of.

**Getting Endorsed for Your Skills**

LinkedIn has a feature that allows your connections to endorse skills listed under the Skills section or even suggest others that you haven't mentioned there. These endorsements are displayed right under the skills mentioned in your profile.

Not every connection is going to endorse your skills, of course. However, since it is easy to endorse someone (simply click on + next to the skill on a profile); connections endorse each other's skills as goodwill gestures.

Ensure your profile is complete and you've listed all skills to make it easier for your connections to endorse them. This definitely boosts your brand's authenticity and credibility. You can delete endorsements that are inaccurate or plain bizarre. Fire eating, anyone?

**Use LinkedIn's Pulse Publishing Platform Optimally**
LinkedIn's Pulse publishing platform gives you a brilliant opportunity to showcase your skills by generating authoritative and useful content and sharing it with your connections.

Updating your LinkedIn blog with regular, valuable, and information-rich content can give you great influencer leverage and present yourself as an industry authority, thus boosting your brand credibility. Keep content relevant to your industry, detailed and analytical, and multi-perspective.

You can also syndicate content from your corporate blog to LinkedIn Pulse, thus drawing a larger audience to your blog.

To publish an article, select Publish a Post. You can also go to Pulse from the Interests option on the main navigation toolbar.

Select Publish a Post once you are done by clicking the top right corner button on the page.

**Make Your Profile More Accessible**
When you visit other profiles, allow them to be able to see your profile, too. Go to Settings and click on your profile image. Click Manage > Profile > Privacy Controls > Select What Others See When You've Viewed Their Profile. Check the Your Name and Headline feature.

**Use Saved Searches**
LinkedIn lets you store a maximum of three people searches and 10 job searches by clicking the Save Search option on the upper right corner. This makes it easy for you to track searches and peruse the information later. Users can get weekly or monthly email reminders when new network users or jobs matching the saved criteria spring up.

**Open Profile for More Connections**
As discussed earlier, only first degree connections can private message each other. This means you can touch base one-on-one with only those customers who are in the same groups as you.

However, there's a way through which you can send other users messages without being a first degree connection. It is called the Open Profile option, and is only available to premium account members.

If you opt for the Open Profile Network, any user (irrespective of their LinkedIn membership or degree of connection) is available to you for one-on-one messaging.

Send an Open Profile Message by clicking on Send an InMail. You can also hover around the top section of the user's profile section and choose Select an InMail. Premium account holders can simply select Send (user's name) and the messaging button.

## Check Out Who's Checking You Out

Just like you want the users of profiles you visit to know about you, you also want to access profiles of users who visit your profile. With the Who's Viewed Your Profile option, accessible within the main navigation in the Profile dropdown, you can view all users who've visited your profile.
Also, LinkedIn has gone a step further and made it even more comprehensive by including a feature where you can actually view how your profile stacks up against your connections' profile views. This opens up a whole new list of potential clients and business associates.

## Optimize Your Profile for Search Engines

Optimize your profile by including key search terms and words that are normally used to describe your profession. The more specific you are, the more likely you are to be found while people search for those terms on search engines.

Include keywords in multiple profile sections, including the profile headline and summary.

LinkedIn allows you to add links to websites within your profile. A neat little tip is to retain links to your other social media pages but change the link text (the clickable words that take visitors to another page) to include more impactful keywords and phrases related to your business.

For instance, your Twitter profile link can read as C++Coder Twitter Profile. This captures the gist of your profile and makes it more optimized for search engines.

**Use the Advanced Search Option**
LinkedIn's Advanced Search option offers a much more focused search experience. For example, maybe you want to know if you are connected to someone who is employed by a specific organization. You simply need to mention the company name and then use the relationships filter for checking if you have any connections with the specific user.

**Cross-Promote by Sharing LinkedIn Updates on Twitter**
Though you can't automatically publish your tweets on LinkedIn, the reverse can be achieved with startling results by adding your Twitter profile to LinkedIn. If you want your Twitter followers to be able to access your LinkedIn updates, syndicate update posts by choosing the Public + Twitter feature under the Share With dropdown option within the update composer.

## New and Existing Connections

The Connections tab in the top navigation offers plenty of features to grow your connections and expand your professional network. Click on Add Connections from the dropdown option to extract contacts using your email accounts and get suggestions and recommendations for more connections. You can connect with others from your university using the Find Alumni function.

Keep in Touch is another unique feature that lets you stay in touch with existing connections, track your communications with them, get notified when they change jobs, and gives birthday reminders.

## Email LinkedIn Groups

Can LinkedIn groups be used to generate leads? Yes, of course. One of the biggest advantages of managing a group is that you can send out messages to each group member (a maximum of once per week). These messages are sent as LinkedIn announcements straight into the inboxes of members, if they enable the 'messages from groups' from their settings.

If you build a thriving group that is packed with insightful discussions, you are tapping into a robust group of targeted customers and associates. You can generate plenty of leads by directing group users to your LinkedIn profile and ultimately to your blog or other social media pages.

Maintain top notch group etiquette by keeping discussions professional and relevant. Rather than focusing on promoting your product, focus on adding more value within the topic so other users can benefit from it.

Once they see you contributing meaningfully to the group, they will automatically take greater interest in your profile, and they will automatically be more receptive to your messages.

**Add Weight to Your Profile**
If you are a fairly new networker or blog owner or business founder, and don't know how to add more weight to your profile, think again! There's plenty that you can put in there to pack more panache into your profile.

It can be anything from knowledge of foreign languages to special volunteer experience to any special projects you've worked on. Since you can add media to your profile too, how about an interesting introductory video that demonstrates your skills?

To add media to your file, Click Edit Profile and select the square icon under Summary and Educations sections. Click to upload media files.

# Conclusion

Thank you for purchasing *Social Media Marketing: A Beginner's Guide to Dominating the Market with Social Media Marketing*.

I hope the book helped you gain invaluable insights about the basics of social media marketing, as well as its little-known, actionable, and practical tips. Using the simple yet effective nuggets of information given in the book, you can come up with your own creative ways to build a powerful online presence for your brand.

The next step is to convert your learning into action. Create a comprehensive social media marketing plan using the expert hints described in the book and implement it confidently. Patience and persistence are the keys to creating stellar social media brands. Take action now and keep going until you see the desired results! You will be surprised!

Lastly, if you enjoyed the book, please take the time to share your thoughts and post a review on Amazon. It'd be really appreciated.

Here's to your powerful social media brands.

Thank you and good luck!

# Free Marketing Blueprint

Marketing can be a complex subject and even after years of experience the same principles still apply.

Give yourself a head start! Grab your free copy of The Marketing Blueprint to help you understand what you need to succeed

To grab your copy of The Marketing Blue Print visit
http://www.mrmarketinghero.com/freebook

# Other Books by Eric J Scott

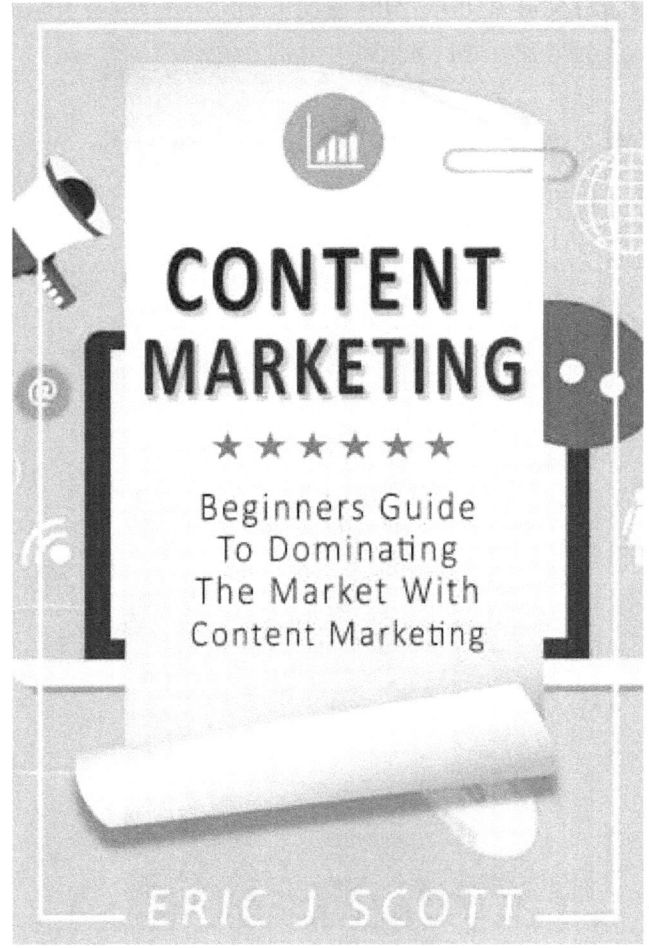

**Content Marketing
Beginners Guide To Dominating The Market With Content Marketing**

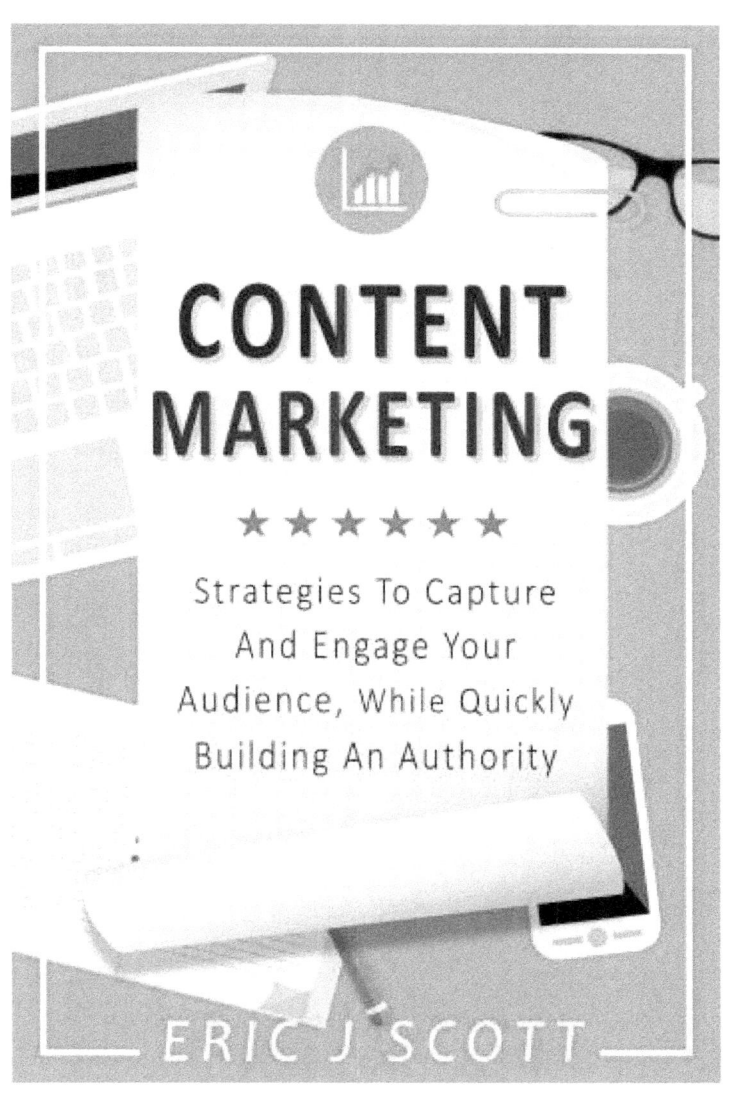

## Content Marketing: Strategies To Capture And Engage Your Audience, While Quickly Building An Authority

# Content Marketing:
# Tips And Tricks To Increase Credibility

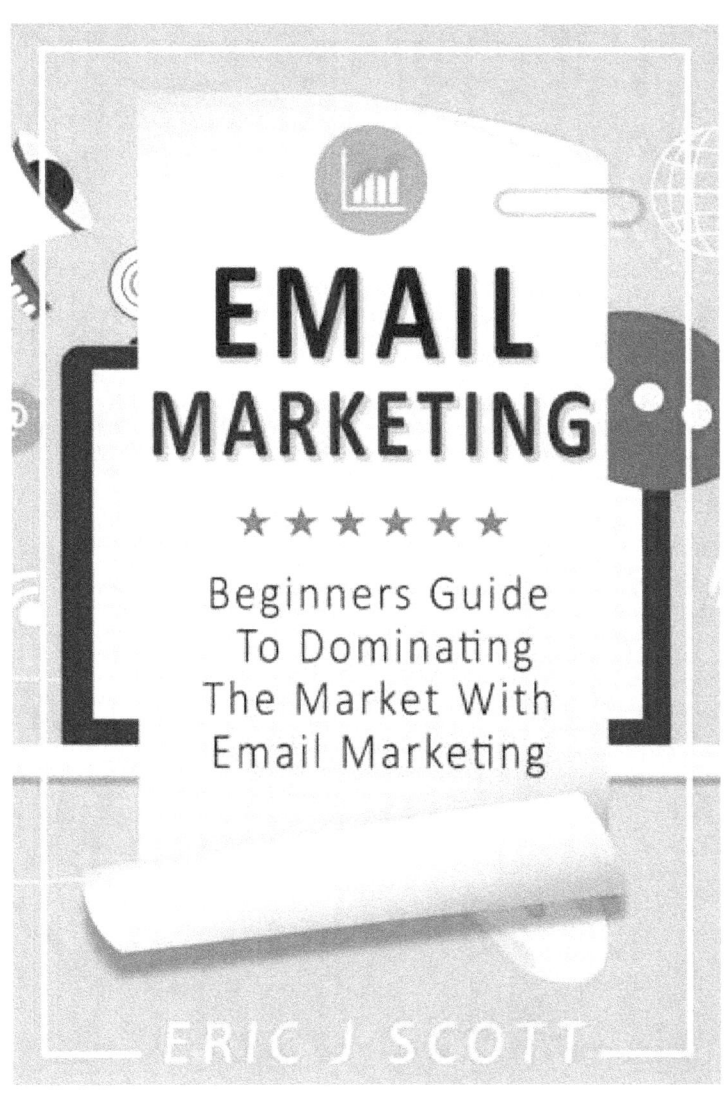

# Email Marketing:
# A Beginner's Guide To Dominating The Market

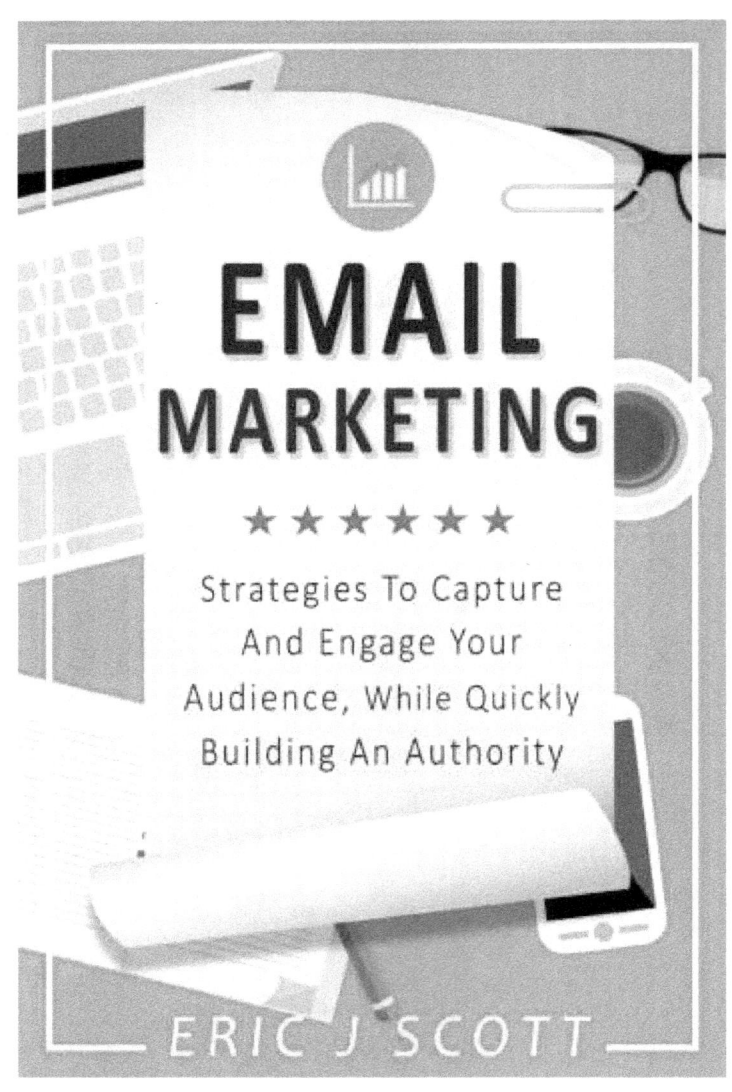

# Email Marketing: Strategies To Capture And Engage Your Audience, While Quickly Building Authority

## Email Marketing: Tips And Tricks To Increase Credibility

# Social Media Marketing: Strategies To Capture And Engage Your Audience, While Quickly Building Authority

# Social Media Marketing:
# Tips And Tricks To Increase Credibility